Philip
Traveling Preacher

JACK NAISH • ILLUSTRATED BY RON HESTER

BROADMAN PRESS
Nashville, Tennessee

Contents

Young Philip

Everyone was busy. There was excitement at Philip's house. Philip's family was getting ready to go to Jerusalem. It was that special time of year when Philip and his family went to the beautiful city of Jerusalem for the Passover.

"Hurry, Mother, hurry," Philip called. "Let's get started."

"Have you packed your clothes and finished those other jobs I gave you to do?" Mother asked Philip.

Philip began to think. *Yes, I've packed my clothes, rolled up and tied my sleeping mat, and filled all the water skins with water. And I also carefully put my gold coins in my small leather pouch.* "Yes, Mother, I've done everything you asked me to do," Philip answered.

"Thank you, Philip. You're a good worker," Mother said proudly. "I needed a good helper like you today."

Remembering the shiny coins in his money pouch, Philip began to think of how special those coins were to him. He had earned the money helping his father in the marketplace. Philip's father was a merchant. Philip had kept the family shop clean and straightened up the various goods. He also watched for thieves who might steal their merchandise. Philip was beginning to understand how important money was and how hard it was to earn.

Philip had saved the coins for this special trip. Perhaps he could give one to the offering for the poor at the Temple service. He wanted to buy a gift for his mother, too, And if there was anything left, maybe a surprise for himself.

"Come on, Philip, let's go," Father called. Philip quickly gathered up his bundles and ran outside to join the others for the journey.

Philip and his family, though they were

Jews, did not live in Palestine. They lived in an area where there were many Greeks and other groups of people. Philip's friends were both Greeks and Jews. Each of them was special, and Philip grew to love them very much.

Because Philip and his family were so much a part of the Greek community, they grew to be different from the Jews in Palestine. Often in Jerusalem Jews from the Greek community were called *Hellenists*, which is a word that means Greeks. They were called Hellenists because they could speak the Greek language as well as the Aramaic language. They acted like Greek people in many ways.

This made some of the Jews in Palestine very unhappy. They felt that the Hellenists were not being true to the teachings of Moses. The strict Jewish leaders taught that it was wrong to make friends with people who weren't Jews. This was difficult for Philip to understand.

Each sabbath, however, Philip and his

9

family faithfully attended the synagogue. His father read faithfully from the Law and the Prophets. Philip was carefully trained in the synagogue school. He learned to read aloud from the Hebrew scrolls, and he memorized special verses. Some of his favorite readings were from the book of Isaiah where the prophet told of the coming of the Messiah. Every night at the evening meal Philip's father prayed that the Messiah might come soon.

Thinkback: The story you have just read is a "maybe" story. "Maybe" it happened, but our Bible does not give us the story of Philip's early life. The Bible does give us some important facts about Philip. These facts are included in the "maybe" story. Do you remember these?

1. Philip probably grew up in a town outside Palestine. He did not grow up in Jerusalem.

2. As a young boy, Philip learned to speak Greek as well as Aramaic. Aramaic

was the language of the Jews in Palestine at that time.

3. Because he was a Jew, Philip probably attended synagogue school.

4. Philip loved all kinds of people.

5. At an early age Philip learned about work and the use of money.

Philip grew up in a city with many kinds of people. He did not dislike others because they were different.

Because Philip loved all kinds of people, God used him to tell people of other countries and cities about Jesus.

How do you feel about people who look, or talk, or act differently from the way you do? Everyone is special to God. Everyone should be special to you.

The Turning Point

Many years had passed. Philip had closed his father's shop in the marketplace. He and his mother, a widow now, were again preparing for a trip to Jerusalem. But this trip was quite different from the ones before. Everything they owned was packed. Jerusalem was to be their new home.

Philip had recently made a wonderful discovery, and his whole life was changed. A few months earlier, on a visit to Jerusalem, an unusual thing happened. Philip heard the wonderful story of Jesus, the Messiah.

Philip was in Jerusalem during the yearly celebration called Pentecost. He was inside the walled city busily buying goods for his shop back home. As he

worked his way through the crowded streets, he came to an open area where the streets joined together. There was a man speaking from the steps of a building. A crowd was beginning to gather as Philip came up.

Philip was curious and stopped to listen. As he became more interested, he worked his way up closer to the speaker.

A hush had fallen over the crowd, for the tall man spoke with great authority. Philip turned to a woman next to him and asked, "Woman, who is the man speaking?"

"Oh, he's one of the followers of Jesus. Some people call him Simon Peter or the fisherman," she replied.

Philip listened carefully that day as Peter spoke. The words were strange to him:

"Jesus is God's Son.
He loved you so much he died for you.
But God raised him from the dead.
He is risen. We have seen him.
He is the living Messiah.
Believe that Jesus is God's Son, be
    baptized, and God will save you
    from your sins."

Peter's words reminded Philip of the longing in his heart for the Messiah. *Could this one of whom Peter spoke be the Messiah, the one my family and I have prayed for through the years?* Philip thought. The words Peter preached were good news to Philip, and he wanted to become a

follower of Jesus. He eagerly accepted that good news and became a part of the group of believers in Jerusalem.

Philip was not the only one who believed. About three thousand other people accepted the good news, believing that Jesus was the Messiah, God's Son.

15

As soon as Philip could get back home, he shared his experience with his mother. They were very excited and happy. Plans were finally made to sell the shop, their house, and many of their possessions. They were going to Jerusalem to live near others who believed Jesus was God's Son.

Thinkback: This section is a "maybe" story also. The Bible does not tell us when Philip came to Jerusalem or when he became a Christian. The Bible does help us know these facts.

1. At some time in his younger life, Philip became a Christian.

2. For a while Philip lived in Jerusalem.

3. He was busy in the Jerusalem church.

For you to think about:

1. Do you believe that Jesus is God's Son?

2. What does being a Christian mean to you?

3. Why is attending church important?

Deacon in the Church

Philip was happy to be with the other Christians in Jerusalem. They came together every day to pray and to hear the apostles teach. Philip was always present, eager to learn more and more about Jesus.

18

19

Day by day the church grew larger and the apostles had to give more and more of their time to feeding the widows and giving out money to the poor. Philip helped them whenever possible.

One evening Peter called the other apostles together and said: "We're spending too much time doing things other than praying and preaching. Yesterday I worked all day at the alms table giving out money. I had no time to pray, and I didn't get to preach the good news of Jesus anywhere. We need to spend our time preaching *and* teaching all over the city."

John spoke up, "Yes and we're also having some complaints from the Greek-speaking widows. They say they are not receiving as much food and money as the Palestinian widows do."

"Why don't we ask the church to choose some good, honest men to help us," Matthew suggested.

"That's a good idea, Matthew," Peter replied. "I'll suggest this to the church

21

tomorrow morning." The apostles prayed together, thanking God for giving them an answer to their problem.

The next day Peter called the church together and said: "Choose seven men from among you to help us in our work. These men should be honest and good. They should be able to work well with all the people. We need to spend our time preaching and teaching."

The church was happy with the suggestion Peter made. One of the members stood and said: "The men we choose need to be good businessmen, too. They will have to handle the money from the offerings for the poor."

Another member stood and said, "Let's choose men who have a Greek background so they can help in a special way with the widows who are not being helped."

"Those are good suggestions," Peter said. "Now, go out and find seven men who are like the ones we have talked about. Look carefully and ask God to

23

guide you."

As the church began to search for the seven men, they chose Philip and Stephen and five others: Procharus, Nicanor, Timon, Parmenas, and Nicolaus.

These seven men became good workers in the church. They had learned well from the apostles and had proven themselves to be honest and faithful followers of Jesus.

When the church gathered again, they brought the seven men to the apostles for their approval and blessing. The apostles prayed for the new leaders and placed their hands on them as a sign of their blessing on their new work.

Philip thought as he prayed quietly, *Jesus, help me be a good worker. Show me how to help others and share the good news of Jesus.*

With the seven men, called deacons, helping the apostles, the church in Jerusalem grew even faster.

Thinkback: Why did the church in Jerusalem need deacons?

24

Can you describe the kind of men the early church chose as deacons?

Do you know a deacon who is a special friend?

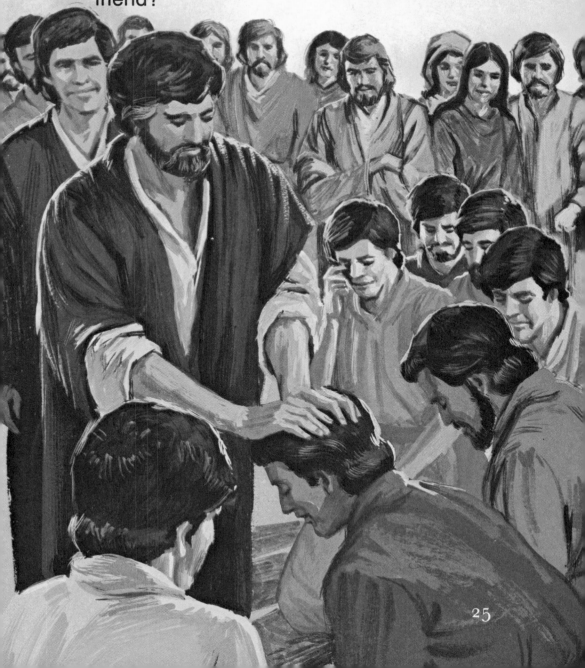

Preacher to the Samaritans

Philip and Stephen became good friends. They often worked together, helping the members of the church.

"Stephen, the church is growing even faster now that we are helping the apostles," Philip said.

"Yes, I know and I'm glad," Stephen replied. "Since we were chosen as special helpers, the apostles have more time for praying and preaching."

"That's the way it should be," Philip agreed.

But as the church continued to grow, Philip and Stephen began doing more than giving out food and money to the poor and needy widows. They began to preach and teach in the synagogues. The people were amazed that Philip and Stephen could perform miracles like the apostles. The power to do such things was given to them by God.

Philip and Stephen spent much of their time working with the Jews who had

moved to Jerusalem from outside
Palestine. Philip and Stephen knew the
language and customs of these Jews.
Philip and Stephen thought they could
share the good news with these men and
women in a special way. Many people
believed the message of the two deacons
and became Christians as they heard the
good news.

One day, however, the leaders of the synagogues became very unhappy with Stephen. "We must stop him," the leaders said. "Too many people are believing that Jesus is God's Son because of what he is saying and because of the miracles he is performing." So they asked some men to tell lies about Stephen. They said, "Stephen is always speaking against the Temple and the law of Moses."

It was not long before guards came and

arrested Stephen. The angry crowd
began to attack him. Dragging him out of
the city, they stoned him to death.

On the day Stephen was killed, a man
named Saul became the leader of the
terrible persecution of the Christians in
Jerusalem. He went into the houses of
Christians, took them out, and put them
in jail.

Philip decided it was no longer safe to

stay in Jerusalem. He thought to himself: *There must be other places where I can witness without being killed or put in jail.* Jerusalem is not the only place to share the gospel.

Possibly Philip had heard from the apostles the words of Jesus, "You must witness for me in Jerusalem, and Samaria, and Judea and all over the world."

Samaria, Philip thought. *That's where I'll go. I'll share the good news with the people there. Jesus said to go there and be his witness.* And Philip began to make plans for his trip.

When Philip arrived in Samaria, the people heard him preach. They saw him heal the sick, and they welcomed him gladly. They were happy to hear the good news of Jesus. They were glad Philip had come to share with them.

The news of Philip's work quickly got back to the apostles. The Jerusalem church wanted to know what was happening in Samaria. They sent Peter and John to check out the wonderful news.

Peter and John stayed in Samaria for a while. They talked with the new Christians and encouraged them. Peter and John also helped Philip preach and teach. Many people became Christians because of their work. As the apostles traveled back to Jerusalem, they stopped at several Samaritan villages to preach the good news to the people there, also.

Thinkback: How did Philip and Stephen help in the Jerusalem church?

What happened that caused Philip to leave Jerusalem?

What were two things that Philip did in Samaria?

A Roadside Sermon

Philip walked along the dusty road to Gaza. He had left Samaria because God had told him to go toward Gaza. *Why did God send me down this way?* Philip kept asking himself. But he knew that God always has a special plan for his workers. He also knew that wherever he went he could preach the good news of Jesus.

The sun was almost directly over Philip's head. It was getting too hot to travel, and Philip had walked a long distance that day.

Just as he came around a curve in the road, there in the distance he could see some trees and green grass. *I'll stop there,* Philip thought. *It will be a good place to rest in the cool of the shade.*

Philip walked faster. As he came closer, he saw a beautiful, silvery chariot parked under the tree. Shiny black horses were tied to one of the tree limbs. Sitting in the chariot was a man dressed in a white tunic and a beautiful red robe. A gold chain, with a large gold emblem was around his neck. *That must be a very important person,* Philip thought.

Walking closer, Philip started to speak to the man. But something made him stop for a moment. The man was reading aloud. *Those are words from the Isaiah scroll.* Philip thought as he listened carefully. *I know those words. My father often read them to me as a child.* Philip remembered his father reading to him from Isaiah about the promised Messiah.

"Hello! My name is Philip. I come from Samaria, and I am on my way to Gaza. I saw you resting here in the shade of the tree. May I join you?"

"Yes," the man said. "I'm returning to my country of Ethiopia. I serve as one of the officials in the court of Queen Candice. My travels have led me to Jerusalem where I went to worship. I'm seeking to learn more about the true God."

"Do you understand what you have been reading?" Philip asked.

"No, how can I?" the Ethiopian answered. "I need someone to explain what it means. Philip, can you help me understand? Come! Sit with me here in my chariot."

Philip climbed into the beautiful chariot and sat down beside the man from Ethiopia. He began to tell him about Jesus. "Jesus is the one Isaiah is speaking of in the scroll." Philip said. "Jesus is the promised Messiah, the Son of God."

The Ethiopian was so happy to hear the good news of Jesus. He said, "Now I understand. Thank you, Philip. Come

34

ride with me." They untied the horses and drove down the dusty road together. As they went, they talked about Jesus and what being one of his followers really means.

Before long they came to some water. The Ethiopian pulled his horses to a stop. "Philip, why can't I be baptized here to show I am a believer in Jesus?" he asked.

Philip said, "You may be baptized if you really believe that Jesus is God's Son.

"Yes, I do believe that Jesus Christ is the Son of God," the Ethiopian said.

He and Philip got down out of the chariot. Down into the water they walked, and Philip baptized him as a new believer of Christ.

"Sir, I must be on my way now!" Philip told the Ethiopian.

"Thank you, Philip, for sharing with me the good news of Jesus." Philip turned down the road as his new friend rode off in the chariot.

Thinkback: What experiences in Philip's early life helped him explain the words of Isaiah to the Ethiopian?

How did Philip learn about the Bible as a young boy?

Do you read your Bible often?

Read the story of Philip and the Ethiopian in your Bible. It is found in Acts 8:26–39.

Settling Down in Caesarea

Philip left the Ethiopian and took the road that led west toward the Mediterranean Sea. As he traveled, he preached in all the cities and villages along the way.

The first city Philip came to was Azotus. Then he traveled north along the seashore to Joppa and Caesarea. Everywhere Philip preached, many men and women believed that Jesus was God's Son.

When Philip stopped in Caesarea, he liked the city very much. It was a large, beautiful seaport town. Ships came in and out of the harbor every day. Philip enjoyed watching the workmen as they loaded and unloaded the big ships. Often he would sit and wonder where the ships

might be sailing next.

As he walked the streets of the city, he met people from faraway places. There were many kinds of people in Caesarea. Philip wanted to share the good news of Jesus with them all.

This will be a good place for me to make my home, Philip thought. *I can preach to the people as they travel back and forth through Caesarea. When they return to their homes, they can share the good news of Jesus with their families and friends!* So Philip settled down and made his home in Caesarea.

As time passed, Philip's family grew. Philip had four daughters. He carefully trained his daughters and taught them about Jesus, God's Son. As his daughters learned to love Jesus, they became Christians and helped Philip in his work.

One morning Philip called to his daughters, "Girls, some very special people are coming to visit us tomorrow."

"Oh Father, who is coming?" the girls asked with excitement.

"I'll tell you later," Philip said. "But first there's much work to be done. We must clean the house, bake fresh bread, and have the best of everything ready for our guests."

That evening when all the work was done, Philip called his family together for the evening meal.

"Thank you God for the food and all the blessings you give us." Philip prayed.

After dinner the girls pleaded, "Father, please tell us who is coming tomorrow."

"All right, girls," Philip said, "I'll see if you can guess. Here is a clue. They are missionaries on their way to Jerusalem."

"Give us another clue, Father," the girls quickly asked.

"One of the missionaries put many of my friends in jail when I lived in Jerusalem. It was before he became a Christian. His name is . . . "

"Paul. It's Paul," the girls said in one big voice. "We'll be so glad when Paul and the others get here. They can tell us all about their missionary journeys."

43

"Yes, I'm sure they will," Philip said. "Now we must go to bed so we will be ready for our guests tomorrow."

Paul and the other missionary friends visited with Philip and his family each time they passed through Caesarea. They enjoyed praying together and sharing with one another how God had helped them in their work.

Philip and his family stayed in Caesarea. Every day Philip preached to the people, and his daughters helped him in his work. They had learned many good habits from their father.

44

Thinkback: Why do you think Philip wanted to preach wherever he went?

Look at the map. Find the cities Philip visited. On the map trace with your finger the route Philip took as he traveled. Begin at Jerusalem. Move over to Gaza, to Azotus, to Joppa, and then to Caesarea.

Why is "traveling Preacher" a good name for Philip?

SOME NEW TESTAMENT PLACES

Reflections

In what kind of ways would you want to be like Philip?
Think about . . .
. . . Reasons God used Philip in so many different ways.
. . . Opportunities you have to help in the work of your church.
. . . How you should feel and act toward someone who is different from you.
. . . Some ways you can share what you know about Jesus.
Remember . . .
In your church today Philip would be called a layman. A layman is a person who works for God and the church, but he is not the pastor or one of the ministers of the church. Some laymen become deacons who help the pastor and the church do their work.
Do . . .
Get to know one of the deacons in your church. Share with him the story you have just read about Philip.